Blackbird

Madeline Brown

BookLeaf
Publishing

India | USA | UK

Presentation by *BookLeaf Publishing*

Web: www.bookleafpub.com

E-mail: info@bookleafpub.com

ISBN: 9789357445191

First edition 2021

DEDICATION

I dedicate this book to Chelita Robinson-Lucas. A woman who always believed in me and always encouraged me to chase my dreams. A beautiful soul gone too soon.

Dreamers:

We're the dreamers of the tomorrow
Thinking of the future; the goals, the rewards
Contemplating our moves
Praying for the light
The knight and shining armor
We kill to get to the bag
Murder to get love.
Stress for the happy days
And long for peace
We're the dreamers of now
Thinking of the present; the plan, the moment
Staying high
Staying lifted
Living for the worst
Hoping for the best
Romanticizing the next
And missing out on our best
But we're the dreamers of yesterday
Thinking of the past; the burdens; the mistakes
Acknowledging our regrets
Growing from our pain
Slaying our demons
Ending our enemies
And washing away our problems

The Pen

It was to me what equations were to a
mathematician.
A cadaver to a surgeon.
It understood me.
It never judged me.
It loved me.
Reassured me.
Believed in me.
It saved me.

It gave me a purpose.
A reason to fall asleep and wake up the next
morning.
It gave me reasons.
A plan.
A couple of goals.
It changed with me.
Grew with me.
It gave me a way out.
An escape.
It gave me… Me.

The Day

Almost a decade but still so fresh.
A day engraved in my brain. In my soul.
Remembering every scream.
Every cry.
Every smell.
Every face.
Every car that passed.
A day that never made sense.
A day where dots didn't connect.
Where stars didn't align.
A day that will replay but not erase.

Scars

She had scars in places no one would see.
She was lost in places no one would find.
She was comfortable with the silence she created
around herself.
Comfortable in the alone.
In the pain.
The scars.
Comfort in herself.

Scared

I'm scared that one day you'll stop telling me
that you love me
And my world would stop spinning.
I'm scared that one day you'll stop holding me
And I'll never feel true comfort again.
I'm scared that eventually, you'll realize you
were always better without me
And I'll never be loved again.
I'm scared one day you'll forget all the little
things
And then I'll be a faded memory.
I'm scared that one day I'll realize I was wrong
And you'll never come back to me.
I'm scared that one day there will be no more
days
And I would have lost you forever.

Holding

You were not someone I wanted to hold on to.
But you became someone I couldn't let go of.
Hard to remember.
Harder to forget.
A dark place.
An odd peace.
An intoxicating feel.
Holding on was never the plan.

Broken

You're not broken, are you?
You're not broken because right now it seems
like your life couldn't be more messed up than it
already is but you're not broken.

You're not broken because you can't seem to
open your eyes and make the right decisions in
life and you choose to live the life of sin but
you're not broken.

You're not broken because every night you
might be crying yourself to sleep over situations
and circumstances that you can't seem to control
but you're not broken.

You're not broken because for the first time in
your life you don't seem to be in control of
whatever it is you're trying to do because you
decided to give your control to someone who
doesn't care but you're not broken.

You're not broken because at this moment in
your life you are weak and sad and out of
control, you are not broken because you refuse

to lay down with the dogs and pout and complain.

You're not broken because even if it takes years on end you'll eventually learn how to get it together.

You are not broken because broken people die and you're still living in all ways even some you don't agree with. You refuse to drown in your sadness, in your stress, in your shame because you are not broken.

You're down right now and the world is on your shoulders but you will never be broken because broken girls don't win and you refuse to lose.

Dad

You were the center of my destruction.
The pinpoint for my heartache.
My pain.
My anger.
Loving you was hard because you made hating
you so easy.
Tears I was left to wipe alone.
Wounds I was left to heal on my own.
Scars I inflicted on others.
You were the center of it all.
Every street leads to you.
I burdened myself with it all.
Feeling everything deeper until there was
nothing.
I was nothing.
But living in my pain didn't relieve you of
yours.
Making myself smaller never made you bigger.
And crying myself at night never made you
come home.

You Gave Me

You gave me everything
The moon, the stars, the clouds
You pushed mountains
And you cleared skies
You gave me clarity
You gave me confusion
You gave me honesty
You gave me lies
Pure bliss
With never-ending pain
Gave me the sun in the morning
The birds in the afternoon
And the pleasure in the evening
You gave me everything
And then absolutely nothing at all
You gave me yourself
And you wanted me
But I wanted myself
You gave me everything
I gave nothing to myself
You picked up broken glass
Cutting yourself on sharpened edges
And blamed me for your blood
Blamed for the battle wounds
And battle scars

I came with a caution sign
But you ignored all the warnings
So you blamed me for the crash
Blamed me for the pain
Blamed me for the hurt
Words you never said
But words you always meant
And so I took the midnight train
To take a break
So you blamed me for the pain
And I broke my back to give you me
And you broke yourself to put me together
I was a puzzle for you
But you were always missing one piece
We gave each other everything
Then absolutely nothing

To My Greatest Love

To my hardest goodbye
To the best part of me
The pain all came in waves
And with every tide, parts of us washed away
You were my sun in the morning
You were my smile
You were my air
But I wanted to suffocate myself
Because that was easier than letting myself be
happy
So now I press a hand just to hear your voice
Now I just wanna waste away in a bottle
Now I just wanna go away forever
Because now I've broken the only good part of
me
I've lost my air
And I drown in my consequences
And now I just hope you find happiness
Even if it's not with me, because I don't deserve
your happiness
I never deserve your happiness, I never deserved
your love.

And to my hardest goodbye
To the greatest man, I know
To my only best friend
I wish you love
I wish you peace
And I'm sorry that couldn't have been me.
For this may be the last of us, you'll always be
my hardest goodbye
And not loving you how you deserved will
always be my biggest failure.

The Dark

It was dark.
Chilling.
Peaceful.
It was familiar.
Honest.
It was new.
But old.
A place I've been before.
A place I would frequent.
It was the only place I knew.
The only place that accepted me.
Always pitch black.
Always comfortable.
Always home.

Expired

We never knew what was harder… falling asleep
or waking up.
We never figured out what caused the most
pain… starting over or keeping it going.
We did know that one day it'll all be clear.
We would finally understand.
We wouldn't call it giving up but giving out.
The days would tire us so that we would make
peace.
We'd make peace with expiring.

Release

She spent a year in a clouded world.
Taking anything at night to feel free of the pain
she felt in the morning.
She found solace in something so small.
Something that calmed the voice.
She took it all… anything she could find.
Anything anyone could give her just to release
her demons.
There was a warning sign on her life.
She saw an expiration date on herself.
She sat on a cold floor… note in one hand, bottle
in the other.
As she seen it all come to an end with no
goodbyes, she got up.

She released it all and got up.
We always got up.

Dedicated to 22-year old Maddy

May 3, 2016

Unhinged since the beginning.
Unorthodox since the start.
We were always different but never far apart.
There was a world I never saw until I saw you.
A life I never wanted to live until I wanted to
live it with you.
A person I never seen myself becoming until I
became it with you.
We drove through storms.
We healed through pain.
We made dark days, shiny weeks.
We did it all.
And with you by my side.
I'd do it again.

Dedicated to Aaron Ashley

Most.

Born through fire and rain.
You had to grow faster than most.
Birth in struggle and heartache.
You had to heal sooner than most.
Danger to yourself and others.
You had to learn control earlier than most.

Your life came at you fast.
Waves hit harder than other days.
Crashing you into the shore.
You drowned faster than most.

You fought harder than most.
Cried harder than most.
Felt harder than most.
Lost more than most.

But we laughed harder than most.
Smiled harder than most.
Succeed more than most.
Lived stronger than most.

We did more than most to be more than most.
And I hope I'm making you prouder than most.

Dedicated to my younger self

Mama

She was stronger than most.
World on her shoulders and her back.
3 kids with one Icon to up too.
She built fences and shifted oceans.
Moved mountains and stopped storms.
Never perfect but always just right.
She built foundations for us to build legacies.

Always the first cheerleader.
Always the first screamer.
Letting us do wrong to let us learn.
Patience was on distant cousin because time had
her moving.
Prideful to her faults.
But always picking herself up.

She made the world spin.
She made the world worth it.
Making each next day worthy.
So what an honor it is
Being hers.

Dedicated to my mother

An Ode to the LOML

To the Love of my Life
My Puerto Rican look alike
The old school pimp
From the hair to the nose
We were one
From the smart remarks to the terrible attitude
I was yours
We lived our best life with family feud
Day parties at the park
Turning up on Chapman street
That Dirty Nickel treated you and the fam good
And The Northside treated us better
So I spent all my free time with you
All the spare time I had was dedicated to you
Because you made all my days shiny and new
And then life got hard
And I ran out of change
So all my sunny days turned blue
Then I lost you
Then there weren't any more colors
All I saw was black
And all I saw was pain

Because my main man had gone away
And it's funny because 2 days before,
You were better
And those blue days turned sunny
And it's funny because a week before, I was just
14
And at the age of 15, my world went black
And I had lost faith
And I had lost hope
Because my main man had gone away
And the pain never ended
And the scars never healed
The void you left would never be filled
Because you were the one who got me through
the sorrow
Who dragged me through the clouds
Who fixed my dark and twisty
And all the moments I wanted to share with you
I might've shared with the bottle
But all my best times were with you
Though the thought of losing you still hurts
The memories of you give me joy
And now I just hope I make you proud
Because with you, there isn't any pain that I
can't through

Dedicated to my grandfather

Brothers

Protectors of my being.
Friends before family.
My very first allies.
My shoulders to lean on.
The wipers of all my tears.
Holding me down and holding me together.
Forever my best men.
Y'all keep me together.
Without you, I'm nothing.
But with you, I'm everything.

Dedicated to my brothers

Easy

Meeting you was hard but loving you was easy.
Complicated but easy.
It came with a certain peace.
It became a daily routine.
Learning who you are as you change.
Adjusting to who you are as you grow.
Loving who you are as you mature.
You were my favorite subject.
And my hard test.

Well Damn

Things untold and things never said.
We lived for each other.
We protected each other.
We choose each other.
We'd sit for hours.
We'd drink for days.
We'd laugh for years.
Grateful for each other.
Never family by blood.
But always family by choice.

Dedicated to my friends

She.

She was legendary before birth.
She was iconic before her first birthday.
Never saying too much but always the loudest in
the room.
A presence that could move mountains.
A smile that tamed men.
Personality that lingered joy.
She was the woman I always wanted to be.
She was me.